Statement Analysis - An ISS Course Workbook

By Steven Varnell

SCV Publishing, Apollo Beach Florida

For information about special discounts for bulk purchases, please contact Steven Varnell at criminalinterdiction@live.com

ISBN 0985382120

ISBN 978-0-9853821-2-4

2 Maccabees 2:32

"At this point, therefore, let us begin our narrative, without adding any more to what has already been said, for it would be foolish to lengthen the preface while cutting short the history itself."

-104 to 63 B.C. in one of the Apocryphal books, which relates the history of Judas Maccabeus

Contents

Prologue

This book was created to accompany my course on Statement Analysis. It can also be used to help anyone understand the importance of analyzing statements made in both the forensic and non-forensic fields. There are countless studies and published reports of new and developing research in analyzing statements. The field is very exciting with continual advancements. Few other lie detection methods are as effective because Statement Analysis explores our use of language which has specific rules to be followed. It is the unconscious violation of these rules which we shall examine.

Today people can use a variety of techniques to enhance their ability to recognize deceit. Most people do not lie about an entire statement, but will "gloss" over the sensitive part that they intend to disguise. This can make recognition of the deception difficult because once completed, they will continue with the truth. We have to determine if they are conveying or convincing. A truthful person will convey the truth. A deceitful person will try to convince you that they are telling the truth.

There is so much material to understand that it requires you to become a regular student of Discourse Analysis. Discourse Analysis is a term for various approaches to analyzing written or verbal communications. I am excited about the possibilities in the field because not only do we study language use, but explore beyond syntax and analyze the natural use of language from different individuals. As with everything, you must study, practice, and use it to stay proficient.

It has been proven that even police officers, are rarely better than chance at detecting deception. My advice is to take as many courses that are available to you and read as many books as possible on these topics. As I always "yell from the rooftop," if you can learn just one thing from any book or class, it was a great book or class. You have been able to add another tool to your toolbox. The more tools in the toolbox, the better prepared you become for any task.

"Society cannot afford investigative interviewing to be poor. This affects people's perceptions of the criminal justice system. The convicted, justice for children and vulnerable adults is inadequate. Poor interviewing is of no value to anyone; it is a waste of time, resources and money. No one wins. People will not come forward if they have no confidence in the quality of investigators' interviewing techniques".

From: Rebecca Milne & Ray Bull.

Investigative Interviewing: psychology and practice.

John Wiley and Sons Ltd: Chichester, 1999, p191.

Statement Analysis - 1

Statement Analysis (SA) is the practice of analyzing a person's words to determine if the subject is being truthful or deceptive via a written statement. Written communication is the preferred examination method of any investigator. It should be attempted before any significant information exchange to commit them into a story. The best analysis comes from the written statement. If unavailable, record the statement for later transcription. Another method prevalent in Europe is for the officer to write it out and the suspect to approve and sign. However, this prevents the very purpose of the process; to allow the person to choose the starting point, what and how to write, and where to stop.

Lying by omission is the preferred method to lie. Liars will tell the truth up to the point where they want to conceal information, skip over the withheld information, and tell the truth again. Successful liars construct sentences that allow them to skip over withheld information to make the story appear truthful. Lies, omissions, half-truths, false leads and the truth may occur in any given statement.

Everyone has a truth bias that they must navigate around when deceit is attempted. By combining truthful parts with lies in a statement, it is difficult for us to recognize. To listen to a statement from a subject, we can easily overlook key elements. Their speech prevents us from recognizing certain characteristics. Placed in written format, and we can analyze the document word for word.

In written narratives, grammar structures are the only mechanisms liars have to link. This is called the truth gap. Since words create sentences and sentence construction follows a pre-determined set of grammar rules, a careful examination of these structures may identify specific sections that signify deception. We use words to define our reality. When we lie, we're trying to adjust two things in our minds at the same time: the real events and the invented or disguised version of them. The language we use reflects that tension and does not follow our normal patterns.

This technique was created by Avinoam Sapir, a former Israeli police lieutenant, based on years of experience interrogating subjects and is only now becoming theoretically based. Sapir calls it Scientific Content Analysis or SCAN, which examines open-ended written accounts where the writers choose where to begin and what to include in the statements. The goal is to highlight areas of a text that require clarification as part of an interview strategy. People will always word their statement based on all of their knowledge of the incident. Therefore, their statement may include information they did not intend to share.

It is nearly impossible to give a lengthy deceptive statement without revealing it a lie. These techniques are very accurate because they are based on the English language, specifically word definitions and the rules of grammar. Many deceptive stories will push the main issue of the statement to the end and does not continue the narrative afterward. They end abruptly or not at all, as if they didn't want to tell the big lie and waited as long as possible to do it. We will see this in Chapter 12 under balancing a statement.

We tend to talk about what is important to us or fresh in our memory. We relive our experiences sequentially in our mind and tend to be consistent and fluid. The most common deceptions are lying by omission and misdirection. This requires someone to think which affects fluidity, consistency, and sequence.

2

To initiate the analysis, have them verbalize why they are there with you! If they are not sure, tell them. It starts them thinking about what to say. It does not mean they are lying, but people have a tendency to just say part of the entire story. No person relates every detail of anything they have experienced. It takes too long. We all "edit" by telling condensed versions deemed important to include in a statement. We also do this in conversation. SA takes into consideration only the words used by the person.

SA can be applied anywhere there is an "open statement," in which the answer is anything the writer chooses. SA deals only with activities and not with intentions and does not deal with what people did, but with what people said that they did.

"I would not do that" while often taken as a denial, is not a denial of past activity. It is a statement of future intent, telling us what the subject would not do. This is not the same as "I have not done …." or "I did not do …."

SA is a tool to help you obtain and evaluate information. To assist in this endeavor, do not use a computer for a written statement. The grammar/spell checker will alter the statement and we want the subject's own words, not those that are grammatically correct. Also, a pen is preferred so corrections can be identified.

A written statement is a narrative relating to an event by the author. Narratives are not unbiased retellings of events, but the reconstruction of the reality based on the authors memory to create meaning to them. They manipulate by selecting or omitting events and changes to get across their point. Therefore, each narrative is evaluated for its clarity and word usage.

After we have confirmed with the subject that they understand the purpose of the interview, explain to them how important it is for them to be completely truthful. There is no gray area. The truth is like being pregnant, you either are or you are not. Let them know that we can work through anything, but we cannot work through a lie. This is the shot across the bow and places pressure against resisting their instinctual truth bias.

Now is the time to have them give you a written statement. Stop everything and let's get the statement in writing. Whether they are a witness, complainant or suspect, get it in writing. This one simple act locks them into their statement. We have already explained to them how important it is to tell the complete truth, now confirm it in writing. Listening to the topic we have the disadvantage of missing critical information. Our ability to listen and analyze every word is very limited. When they are writing, they will concentrate on the exact wording they believe will allow their story to be accepted. We can then analyze this written statement word for word to see where it fails.

We are always seeking discrepancies in specific word use, syntax, tense, verb and pronoun use, adverb and adjective use, clarity, contextual information, reproduction of conversation, perceptual and affective information, balance, negations, segmentation markers, and transitional wording. The remaining sections of this book will cover these areas of concern.

Statement Dissections - 2

It always starts with the statement. Read it sentence for sentence, word for word. Examine their word usages for normality's. When you see the abnormal word usages, they will stand out like a beacon. Read the following statement and analyze for discrepancies.

"Around 5:00am / 5:30am I was in the process of giving my son his scheduled feeding. During this feeding he bucked & fell approx. 2ft. to the floor, hitting his head on the floor. His body landed head first; I attempted to catch him but was unsuccessful. When I picked him up he cried for about 90 sec. then started to gag. His eyes were glazed. I immediately called 911."

What catches my eye with this statement is the fathers' use of the noun "body" to name his son before he hits his head. This demonstrates that the son is already dead and falsifies the statement.

"Around 5:00am / 5:30am I was in the process of giving my son his scheduled feeding. During this feeding he bucked & fell approx. 2ft. to the floor, hitting his head on the floor. His **_body_** landed head first; I attempted to catch him but was unsuccessful. When I picked him up he cried for about 90 sec. then started to gag. His eyes were glazed. I immediately called 911."

Now examine the following statement from a traffic crash.

"I saw the stop sign. Before I entered the intersection, I looked both ways, drove into the intersection and was struck in the right passenger door by the other vehicle."

I prefer to break a statement down to episodic markers of time, place, and punctuation markers. These will be explained later as transitional words and episode markers.

1. I saw the stop sign.
2. Before I entered the intersection,
3. I looked both ways,
4. Drove into the intersection and
5. was struck in the right passenger door by the other vehicle.

The writer has explained each action taken except one. Do you see it?

We are not told if the driver stopped at the stop sign.

A witness said that the motorist did look both ways at the intersection, but he did not stop at the stop sign. In reality, the motorist did see the stop sign. He did look both ways before entering the intersection, and the other vehicle did strike the motorist's passenger side door; however, the motorist failed to write that he did not stop at the stop sign. The motorist used the Text Bridge "before" to bridge the withheld information with the truth. We will discuss Text Bridge's in Chapter 6.

People always mean exactly what they said. "I am trying to be honest." The speaker is telling us that they are not being honest. The word "tried" means to only attempt to be truthful. When a rape victim uses the pronoun "we" in her statement regarding her attacker, this shows plurality and a partnership was formed. This is not an expected word usage. We can think of many expletives, but not a union. Vice versa, we shall also see where an accused rapist will use the phrase "she and I" instead of "we" when trying to convince that it was consensual.

President Obama said to the small business owners of the country:

"Somebody invested in roads and bridges. If you've got a business — you did not build that."

There are two subject matters in this statement based upon the sentence closing;

1- roads and bridges,
2- a business.

We were told that he was referring to the roads and bridges. If true, then he would be required to use "those" instead of "that." "That" is singular specific and can only refer to "a business," the only singular object in the sentence.

Sometimes, the writer will complete the statement with admission's that there is more information concerning a certain topic or issue which has not yet been divulged. These are called unfinished business statements. In SA, we can recognize these occasions with the word usages of:

"That's about it."

"That's about the size of it."

"That's about all."

There are admissions that certain information cannot be given at the moment for whatever reason. Deception exists concerning the topic which precipitated the response. They are demonstrated by the use of the words:

"I can't say."

"I can't think of anything."

"I can't tell you anything about that."

"I can say this ...."

"I can only tell you this ......"

When a speaker uses the conditional verbals of could, would, should or ought to preface a verbal response, remember that these are indicative of future intent. They are often used in hypotheticals. However, if something is hypothetical then it is not occurring in the present and cannot have occurred in the past. These words are confused by most people as referring to past events. "I could have done..." is not saying what has happened, but what may happen next time.

Rambling chatter is often used as a smokescreen. Keep them on topic. The answer that does not equate to what was specifically asked is the most common tactic used by politicians. They will espouse many long sentences and never answer the question.

But - Behold the Underlying Truth; whenever you see the word or a synonym of "but" - however, then, nonetheless, then again, yet, still, although, though, anyway. These words withdraw the previous assertions. Pay attention to what follows.

The word "this" indicates closeness while the word "that" shows distance. However, people will use the wrong word such as:

"I walked into the room and saw this gun and immediately ran out." The "this" gun referred to in the statement was on the other side of the room. The phrase should have been "that gun" to indicate they saw the gun and ran out. "This gun" says they were close to the gun and had entered further than stated.

SA examines language based deception; therefore we should take each statement or sentence into account. (Lies, omissions, half-truths, false leads and the truth may occur) Remember, they will tell you what they want and much of what they say will be true, but true of what? This is known as Millers Law. Miller's law is part of a theory of communication formulated by George Miller, Princeton Professor and psychologist. It instructs us to suspend judgment about what someone is saying so we can first understand them without instilling their message with our own personal interpretations. We can accept that what they tell us is true, but determine what is it true of? The law states:

"To understand what another person is saying, you must assume that it is true and try to imagine what it could be true of."

The point is not to blindly accept what people say, but to do a better job of listening for understanding. It helps to prevent bias. "Imagining what it could be true of" is another way of saying to consider the consequences of the truth, but to also think about what must be true for the speaker's "truth" to make sense. This initial acceptance of the truth is essential to help prevent false interpretations. When we initiate the interview with the belief they are lying, this bias can cause us to falsely read between the lines.

Understanding Syntax - 3

A statement must have:

- structure and length
- text coherence
- factual and sensory detail
- word or phrase structure choice
- verbal immediacy - refers to the degree of separation created between the speaker and the object of their communication as a result of the particular words used by the speaker. "you and I" is considered non-immediate because it uses two symbols ("you" and "I") to designate two separate entities when ("we") could have been used.

Statement Analysis has been enhanced with the understanding that truthful statements include sensory information. Deceptive statements will often lack contextual (time and location), perceptual (sensory), and affective (feelings or thoughts) information. We must examine each word within every sentence to see how it correlates with the topic. Clarity is a must. When we are telling a story from memory, we can explain so it flows naturally. There should not be continual episodic segmentations or short sentences which are steadily changing.

Analyze the verb tenses in a statement. When a person is telling us what happened, they are required to speak in the past tense

"I _am_ sitting in my car when a man opened my door, pointed a gun at me and **_tells_** me to get out of the car."

The words "am" and "tells" are present tense. We cannot recount a past activity in present tense. It can <u>only</u> be in the tense that we remember it for it to be real.

Indefinite articles, "a" or "an" are used when something or someone is first introduced. Once used, it change's to "the."

"**_A man_** approached me and pointed **_a gun_** at me. He stuck **_the gun_** in my ribs and forced me into **_the car_**."

"The gun" was already introduced and is correct with "the". "The car" is the first time it is mentioned. Either it did not happen or "the car" was recognized, therefore using "the" correctly.

"I went shopping with my wife."

"With" in a statement can mean distance. "I" in the beginning and "wife" at the end, then add in the "with" means I was not happy about shopping. There is separation in the statement.

"My wife and I went shopping."

The word "and" attaches us together. We say what we mean because we do not think about everything we say.

President Bill Clinton said, "I was bound to be truthful and I tried to be." "Tried" means attempted or he attempted to be honest, but was not.

"Never" cannot be used to replace the word "no". It is only appropriate on its own to advise the issue has not ever occurred.

Example: "Are you transporting drugs?"

"I would never do that!"

They are not saying no because they mentally cannot. They also included the futuristic word "would" which tells us; "In the future I will not transport drugs."

A yes or no question demands a yes or no answer. If not, some type of deception has occurred.

Q- Are there drugs in the car?

A- "I would never have drugs."

How many problems exist in this brief sentence?

1 - This is a question that asked for a yes or no answer.

2 - They used the word "never" which is not a substitute for no.

3 – "Would" shows future intentions; present tense is "I do not have any drugs."

Connie Chung interview of Congressman Gary Condit in regards to his missing intern, Chandra Levy.

1. Chung: Do you know what happened to Chandra Levy?
2. Condit: No, I do not.
3. Chung: Did you have anything to do with her disappearance?
4. Condit: No, I didn't
5. Chung: Did you say anything or do anything that could have caused her to drop out of sight?
6. Condit: You know, Chandra and I never had a cross word.
7. Chung: Did you kill Chandra Levy?
8. Condit: I did not

In this exchange, we can see how Condit's answers are initiated and completed based on the question asked except once. In line 6, the answer to line 5 changes pattern and indicates concern. We later learned that they had had an affair which he broke off causing her to run away. She was murdered by another person, but Condit felt guilty over their argument.

Joran Van der Sloot on the murder of Stephany Flores in Peru:

"Yes, I want to plead guilty. I wanted from the first moment to confess sincerely. I truly am sorry for this act. I feel very bad."

1. "Yes, I want to plead guilty." (I want to but cannot. Different from I am guilty)
2. "I wanted from the first moment to confess sincerely." (Again he is not saying he confesses he just says he wanted to)
3. "I truly am sorry for this act." (This act but not others. He got caught this time)
4. "I feel very bad. "

The entire statement is narcissistic or about himself, not the crimes he committed or the victims he left behind

Current Research shows there are 12 linguistic indicators of deception cited in the psychological and criminal justice literature to be considered for each sentence in a statement. We are always watching for a lack of commitment to a statement. This occurs when they use linguistic devices to avoid making a direct statement of fact.

- Linguistic hedges - whose meaning implicitly involves fuzziness, e.g., maybe, I guess, and sort of. Hedging shows a lack of commitment.
- Qualified assertions, which leave open whether an act was performed, e.g. I needed to get my inhaler (Was it used?), I wanted to find a weapon. (Did you?) (Uncompleted action verbs)
- Unexplained lapses of time, e.g. later that day
- Overzealous expressions, e.g. I swear to God
- Rationalization of an action, e.g. I was unfamiliar with the road.

Preference for negative expressions in word choice, syntactic structure (rules of combining words to create sentences) and semantics (word meanings).

- Negative forms, either complete words such as "never" or negative meanings as in "inconceivable."
- Negative emotions, e.g. I was a nervous wreck.
- Memory loss, e.g. I forget.

Inconsistencies with respect to verb and noun forms

- Verb tense changes
- Thematic role changes, e.g. changing the theme role from specific name (Cindy) in one sentence to patient or she in another.
- Noun phrase changes – person, place or thing.
- Pronoun changes – they, he, she, we

The following is a transcript of an oral statement from a college student who reported that a man broke into her apartment at 3:30 am and raped her.

"He grabbed me and held a knife to my throat. And when I woke up and I was, I mean I was really asleep and I didn't know what was going on, and I kind of you know I was scared and I kind of startled when I woke up, you know, you know I was startled and he, he told, he kept telling me to shut up and he asked me if I could feel the knife."

Watch for anything that stands out or is odd. As you can see, it is easier if we break the statement in separate items.

1. He grabbed me and
2. held a knife to my throat.
3. And when I woke up and
4. I was, I mean I was really asleep and
5. I didn't know what was going on,
6. and I kind of you know I was scared and
7. I kind of startled when I woke up,
8. you know, you know I was startled and
9. he, he told, he kept telling me to shut up and
10. he asked me if I could feel the knife.

What stands out in this statement is the word usage for the situation. Line 7 shows us that she was "kinda of startled?" Imagine yourself, male or female, waking up at 3:30 am and seeing a man at your bedside holding a knife at your throat. Would you be startled or scared sh..less!

Changes in Tense - 4

The questions asked needs to be in the proper past or present tense. In this example, we are able to guide them to the correct answer by recognizing their improper use of present tense wording.

Q – "Have you ever smoked marijuana?" Past tense

A – "I don't use drugs." Present tense

Q – "That was not the question, have you ever?"

A - "I have tried it once."

"It happened Saturday night. I went out on my back deck to water the plants. It was almost dark. A man <u>runs</u> out of the bushes. He <u>comes</u> onto the deck, <u>grabs</u> me and <u>knocks</u> me down."

Past tense narratives are the norm for truthful accounts of past events. However, it is deviations from the past tense that often correlate with deception. These changes in tense can be more indicative of deception than the overall choice of tense, even though each can demonstrate error.

Investigating an accident, both drivers claim it is the others fault. Each is asked to give written statements.

D1 – began by describing activities using past tense. "I was driving... looking at the scenery. I didn't think much of it...I was not blocking traffic. She had plenty of room...she moved alongside of me and stayed there.... When I glanced in her direction, she looked at me like I was dirt. We drive like this for some time and then she cuts right in front of me. I don't see her coming until it's too late. We pulled off the road and she started screaming that I ran into her."

Notice the tense change at the critical point of the statement, "she looked at me like I was dirt." It is at this moment that the reason for the accident has occurred and his use of tense moves to present. This is indicative that he told the truth up to this point and lied at the critical point and then reverts back to past tense.

"We ***drive*** like this for some time and then she **cuts** right in front of me. I ***don't*** see her coming until ***it's*** too late. We pulled off the road and she started screaming that I ran into her."

Look at the statement by Susan Smith who left her little boys strapped into her car and rolled it into a lake. She claimed that she was carjacked and the kids kidnapped.

"I just feel hopeless, I can't do enough. My children wanted me. They needed me. And now I can't help them. I just feel like such a failure."

Break the statement into individual sentences for better recognition of deceptions.

"I just **feel** hopeless,

I **can't** do enough.

My children **wanted** me.

They **needed** me.

And now I **can't** help them.

I just **feel** like such a failure."

When speaking about herself, she phrases the sentences in present tense. When speaking of her children, she phrases them in past tense and returns to present tense for herself. She knows her children are dead.

Self-Referencing Pronouns, Adverbs and Adjectives - 5

Studies of deception have found that deceivers tend to use fewer self-referencing expressions (I, my, mine) than truth-tellers and fewer references to others. When someone is relating a story that they are involved in, their commitment is usually expressed with the pronoun "I."

"I got up at 7:00 when my alarm went off. I took a shower and got dressed. I decided to go out for breakfast. I went to the McDonald's on the corner. I finished breakfast and drove to work."

Now look at the same statement again to see the area of concern.

"I got up at 7:00 when my alarm went off. I took a shower and got dressed. I decided to go out for breakfast. I went to the McDonald's on the corner. Met a man who lives nearby. Talked with him for a few minutes. I finished breakfast and drove to work."

Scott Peterson's initial police interview is characterized by a high number of omitted first person references:

BROCCHINI: You drive straight home?

PETERSON: To the warehouse, dropped off the boat.

So was Levi Aron murder confession of a missing NY City boy.

"A boy approached me on where the Judaica book store was. He was still there when went out from the dentist's office. He asked me for a ride to the Judaica book store."

Possession Pronouns requires: my, his, hers.

Responsibility is indicated by: I, he, and she. We, us, and they shows plural involvement. "I" is a necessity for a person's statement to be believable. It shows commitment in the statement.

Contrary to The first statement that deception can be indicated with a lack of self-referencing pronouns, too many can be as bad. This will be shown in Chapter 11.

We have already seen how the self-referencing pronoun "I" is important to the commitment of the story. When and how it is used versus the plural first person referencing pronoun "we" also tells variations to a story.

A young woman who reported that she had been abducted at a shopping center provided the following written statement:

"I parked and started getting out of my car when a white male about 200 pounds 6 feet tall approached me and told me to get in the car or he would hurt me. He then got in   the back. I got in the front and began to drive. He told me to drive west on the highway. He asked me if I had any money. I told him no. We drove for about an hour. During that hour, he hit me repeatedly on the right side of my face. When we got to the exit, I told him I had no gas. He got mad and told me to get off the exit. We went straight off the exit for about 4-5 miles. He told me to turn down the first street on my left. We went down it about 1/4 of a mile. He told me to stop. He opened the door, put both feet out, hit me, and took off walking quickly. He took off to the east of where I was parked. After that, I took off and lost sight of him."

Look this statement over and make a determination if there are any issues.

A true abduction statement includes phrases like "He forced me to drive..." or "He made me get off at the exit...." Traumatized victims who are telling the truth do not use the pronoun "we" to describe assailants and themselves. Identify other errors in the statement.

Any time you see an 'ly or y" adverbs connected to a statement (examples-basically, very etc.) Try to recognize this as a potential area of sensitivity and explore. Always watch for the words "actually", "really" and "basically" in a statement. They are synonymous with each other and used to indicate a summation of the most important aspects of a more complex situation have been undertaken. They are used to bolster a sentence, but it usually weakens it. In writing, less is more. Consider the following statement from Casey Anthony's 911 call:

CA: My daughter has been missing for the last 31 days.

911: And you know who has her?

CA: I know who has her. I've tried to contact her.

CA: I actually received a phone call today. Now from a number that is no longer in service.

We see in the last statement that she uses "actually" to say she had received a call today. People are always trying to either convince or convey. Actually is synonymous with really and basically. They are 'ly adverbs that are unnecessary and therefore used to try and convince someone that what is being said is the truth. The truth needs only to be conveyed.

Every study indicates that an excessive use of adverbs and/or adjectives is symptomatic of deception.

TEXT BRIDGES - 6

When a person uses phrases such as "later on" or "afterwards" they have withheld some information by skipping over something in the story. This is considered hedging or a text bridge and is non-committal to the statement. Text bridges allow people to transition from one topic to another without tedious details. For example, in the sentence "I got up, and then I took a shower, and then I ate breakfast," the text bridge "then" signals withheld information. The withheld information does not have to constitute deception. The writer did not want to bore the listener with all of the extraneous information and "jumped" over it. However, text bridges used at critical times during interviews may signal deception.

The most commonly used text bridges are: **then, so, after, when, as, while, and next.** The second most used are: **once, finally, afterwards, eventually.**

Memorize this list of text bridges and you will have a powerful tool to identify where people withhold information during interviews or conversations.

Adverbial conjunctions, transitional and subordinating words are all text bridges. Adverbial conjunctions transition from one idea to the next. A transitional word connects themes and ideas or establishes relationships. Subordinating words connect independent and dependent clauses. They also connect unequal but related ideas and create time gaps.

For a complete list of Text Bridge words, refer to Chapter 13.

"It rained on Saturday; therefore, the picnic was canceled."

The idea that it rained was connected to the idea of the canceled picnic with the transitional word "therefore." They can both separate and connect ideas.

"During the break I drank a soda."

"During" brings the ideas of a break and drinking a soda together.

"We went bowling instead of going to the movies."

The transitional word "instead" contrasts the act of going bowling and the act of going to the movies.

What is the text bridge in the following sentence?

"Mary went to the store and then she went home."

The adverbial conjunctive "then" connects the first complete idea, "Mary went to the store," with the second complete idea," she went home."

A husband suspected of killing his wife arrived home at 5:00 p.m. and made the following statement to the investigating detective,

"After I came home, I found my wife dead."

Is there a text bridge in this sentence to require further examination?

The subordinating word "after" creates an information gap from the time the man came home until the time he found his wife dead. The murder suspect wanted to give the impression that he arrived home and immediately found his wife dead. The murder suspect arrived home at 5:00 p.m. but did not indicate what time he found his wife dead. A time gap exists from 5:00 p.m. until the suspect found his wife dead. During this information gap, the murder suspect got into an altercation with his wife and killed her. The murder suspect hid the physical altercation with his wife by using the text bridge" after."

The following illustration demonstrates how text bridges function. A student wrote a statement in response to allegations that' she took $20 from her instructor's office during the first class break. Pursuant to an informal investigation, the student wrote a narrative account of her activities from the time she entered the building until the end of the first break. The following is a copy of her statement:

"I arrived at 7:45 a.m. with Jenna. I came into the room, put my bag at my desk and Jenna and I went to the little snack area to get some coffee. I returned to the classroom and sat at my desk. At 8:50 we went on a break. Jenna and I went to the bathroom. After that I came back to the classroom and Jenna stayed in the bathroom. She came back to the classroom soon after. We sat at our desk and waited for our class to continue."

Identify the truth gap.

"After" is the text bridge used to give the statement a temporal lacuna or time gap. This is the point where she disguised her actions of going to the office and stealing the money.

Text bridges used at critical junctures during interviews or written narratives signals that the interviewee intentionally or unintentionally withheld information. Text bridges indicate missing information. If the withheld information is of no value, then we can ignore the text bridge. For example, if the crime occurred at 8:00p.m., the suspect may be directed to write a narrative relating his activities from the time he woke up until the time he went to sleep.

"At about 7 o'clock that night, I went to a friend's house for a while and then I went directly home."

The text bridge "then" is significant because the writer created a temporal lacuna (time gap) between 7 o'clock and the time the writer arrived at home. In this case, the suspect probably committed the crime after he left his friend's house but before he arrived home. By using a text bridge, the suspect avoided telling a lie. The suspect did go to his friend's house at 7 o'clock and the suspect did go home. The suspect failed to mention the fact that he committed the crime between the time he left his friend's house and the time he went home.

It has already been shown that liars use fewer words in a statement. In addition, the number of text bridges is also indicative of deception. To determine the number of text bridges in a statement, you can divide the total number of text bridges in a statement by the total number of words to produce a text bridge ratio. This can be helpful when there is no truthful narrative to use as a comparison.

Negations and Opposites - 7

Negations and spontaneous negations are similar to a text bridge and can be recognized by the variations of the word "no." Examples are, no, no one, none, nothing, contractions with the word no, isn't, can't, hasn't, haven't, etc. It also includes the word "never." They fail to state what specific actions the suspect took.

Did you rob the store?

No, I did not rob the store.

This is a negative answer to a direct question and appropriate when used directly in response to a yes or no question.

Spontaneous negations are used when people are presented with open-ended questions. They should relate the actions they took versus the actions they did not take.

(Statement from a rape/murder case)

"Did you want to kiss her?"

"I...I...I didn't feel...I didn't remember feeling any attraction to her. " (The exact opposite is usually true)

Negations are words that negate part or all of a sentences meaning. We have to also watch for their excessive usage with words like, no, never, no one, nothing, not.

Negators or negative words have prefixed verbs by adding "un-" such as unsuccessful. Other negators are – a-, de-, dis-, in-, mis-, and –less. These produce passive language to help separate the speaker from the action.

Words with equivalent opposites require two or more words to complete their definitions. The word "upstairs," cannot be defined without the word "downstairs." The word "hot" cannot be defined without the word "cold." Some words need more than two words to complete their meanings. The word "medium" cannot be defined without the words "large" and "small." The word "warm" cannot be defined without the words "hot" and "cold."

If someone says, "I don't remember," the listener can presume that in order for the speaker to not remember something, he must have had to remember it first. The same logic applies to the responses, "I don't recall" and "I forgot. "

Dad: What did you do last night?

Daughter: I went to the library and then I came straight home.

The text bridge "then" signals missing information, which does not necessarily mean the daughter, is lying. You should inquire further to verify. Look at the opposite of the word "straight." It is conjoined with the word "crooked." After further talking, the daughter admitted going to the library, but for only a few minutes. A temporal lacuna was exposed with the word "then" and was intensified with the word straight. After leaving the library, she admitted to going to a party.

In the last Chapter we saw the statement:

"At about 7 o'clock that night, I went to a friend's house for a while and then I went directly home."

We know that the text bridge is the word "then." We also see in this sentence the opposition word "directly" which like "straight," has an opposite, "indirectly."

Passive Language and Uncompleted Action Verbs - 8

Passive voice or language is when we try to place blame elsewhere or to someone to distance themselves. The husband of a woman who had disappeared wrote in his narrative about the incident that "it was determined that I would drop her off to run." Instead of writing, "I determined" or "we determined," the husband used passive voice or an unknown of "it was determined."

Good follow-up questions to this situation are:

- You wrote that "it was determined that I would drop her off to run." Can you explain this to me?
- Who exactly "determined" that you would drop her off?
- Where was Michelle when "it was determined"?
- Did Michelle participate in the decision to drop her off?

Other examples of a passive voice are using the words someone, somebody, anyone etc.

In an effort to camouflage their deeds, people occasionally use "uncompleted" action verbs or words that denote reference to activity on the part of speakers or writers without any indication that this action was completed. Some of the more common words that fall into this category include ***started***, ***commenced***, ***initiated***, and ***proceeded***. These words reveal the possibility that something or someone interrupted the action and, therefore, warrant scrutiny.

The husband from the last case was asked to write what he knew about his wife's disappearance. He responded,

"Michelle put a workout tape in the VCR and started her workout. I was in the bathroom for a while getting ready for the day."

The word "started" should capture your attention. It shows that something may have interrupted the workout and required some follow-up questions.

- You wrote that "Michelle put a workout tape in the VCR and started her workout." Can you tell me more about this?
- How long did the workout last?
- Where were you when she started her workout?
- You stated that you were "in the bathroom for a while." How long was "a while"?
- What did you do in the bathroom?
- Did Michelle finish her workout?
- Did something interrupt her workout?

The husband eventually admitted strangling her after an argument and dumped her body.

Another example of an uncompleted action verb:

The following is a portion of a statement from a deputy who reported that he was assaulted by an inmate in a court lock-up facility. This is a partial statement surrounding the description of the assault.

Was the deputy actually punched?

"...I then held his shoulders and began to direct him to a seating position, while continuing to try to talk him into compliance. He shifted his body laterally to avoid being directed into the seating posture, arching his back & struggling against me. While I continued to push on him, he was able to punch the right side of my face in the vicinity of my nose and eye..."

He did not say "he punched the right side of my face." He said the inmate "was able to." Clarity through additional questioning is required.

As we have seen, people may hide their actions by using passive voice, or include uncompleted action verbs. With our recognition of these actions we can focus our questions appropriately.

"The pistol was fired by someone."

- Tell me about the pistol being fired. Did you fire it?

"I started to pack my bags."

- Who or what interrupted?
- You said you "started to pack your bag." Did you finish packing?
- Did something interrupt you?

Words That Convey Conversation - 9

We must pay attention to words that convey dialogue. Once recognized, we will want to direct our questions to fill in the conversation. Examples, Talked, spoke, chatted, discussed, and e-mailed.

- What was the conversation about?
- When did the conversation occur in relation to the crime?
- Who did the conversing?
- Were different words used to describe any conversation and, if so, why?
- Were different words used to describe any conversation with the same person or with another person?

Specific Questions regarding conversation

- Tell me what you talked about.
- Was this talk cordial, emotional, angry?
- When did you two talk? What time was it?
- Who else was present when you talked?
- Who might have overheard you?
- What happened after you talked?
- Who initiated the talk?
- Who said what to whom?
- You said, "He and I talked." Tell me about this.

- You said, "We chatted." Tell me more about this chat.

Some words are used that act as a camouflage that a communication occurred. Some examples are; met for coffee, ate lunch, and watched TV. People typically engage in verbal interaction during social activities. Once recognized, specify your questions for clarity.

- What was discussed during the activity?
- Tell me about your meeting for coffee. What did you talk about?
- When did you meet?
- Who else was there?

Backward Reaching Questions or Micro-Action Interviewing - 10

"I went to the bedroom. After leaving the bedroom, I left for work. After arriving at work, I met with my boss."

Guilty persons will often practice deception by omitting information they believe will incriminate them. Leaving out these details is a common way to mislead investigators because technically, it is not lying. It also does not produce as much stress as telling an outright falsehood. Once these text bridges are recognized, you must force closed the time gap. With each question you can close it further until it is fulfilled.

Get a written statement and examine each sentence in the initial narrative for indicators of missing information.

The opening scenario contains four potential areas of omitted details:

1) What happened in the bedroom?

2) What the suspect did after leaving the bedroom before departing for work;

3) What occurred on the way to work; and

4) What transpired after arriving at the office before meeting with the boss?

Although these details may not be important, you should not take the chance.

Once a temporal lacuna is recognized it should be addressed. Also, note the areas of the statement which caused a pause. There may be numerous words marked out, letters written over and show as much darker, or maybe a period which is too dark.

First, return them to the exact point in the narrative where a possible omission of information began. Have them restate word-for-word the information directly preceding the omission; it is important to use the exact language used by the subject. Then, have the suspect expand on the previous information, ensuring that they identify any additional gaps in time and missing details.

Some interviewers make the mistake of going directly to the areas of greatest interest. Instead, they should proceed chronologically, beginning with and closing the first area of omission and patiently moving on to the subsequent areas. By doing so, interviewers avoid alerting the subject to specific areas of interest. In interviews, at least two people are seeking information—the investigator and the interviewee.

From the earlier statement, "I went to the bedroom. After leaving the bedroom, I left for work. After arriving at work, I met with my boss." we can follow up by asking:

- "Earlier you said that you went to the bedroom. What did you do next?"

"Next" would force the subject to discuss the subsequent period of time with either the truth or a descriptive lie. Interviewers also could close the same omission by asking,

- "You said you went to the bedroom and that later you left. Tell me everything you did while in the bedroom."

If a subject says, "That is basically what happened" or "That is about it," you should consider that the interviewee has more to say. Follow up by reaching back and restating the exact words used to compose the original statement:

"Mr. Jones, a few moments ago, you said that is about all you can remember. What else happened at the meeting, or what else do you remember?"

The same technique can effectively address qualifiers. With the statement "I have no specific recollection," ask, "Earlier, you said you had no specific recollection. What recollection do you have?"

These are backward-reaching questions and can address a noncommittal phrase, such as "I cannot remember." The interviewer could ask,

"Mr. Jones, earlier, you said that you do not remember who was present at the meeting. Take a moment and think hard about the meeting again and tell me everyone who was present."

Example:

"Tell me about the last time you saw your wife."

"I recall that, ah, it was one evening, probably 11 o'clock. We were both in bed and we had not gone to sleep yet and she got out of bed. I, ah, thought she was probably going to the bathroom and then I hear the, ah, front door close and I waited for a minute to see what she was doing and then I hear the car start and I look out the window and see the car disappearing around the corner and that's the last time I ever saw her."

Using the backward reaching questions or micro-action interviewing in which we back our line of questioning to the point just prior a text bridge and fill in the gap. Use as many questions as is necessary to satisfy the time period. As they talk use verbal continuators to keep them moving; "What happened next?" If they skip over another part, you have to move the questioning back to prior of the bridge and continue.

Truthful people may find the process tedious, but will continue to answer and add info. Liars will struggle as the time gap is reduced. They will struggle to find words to fill in the gap. This is a good location to ask other questions such as.

- "You were pretty mad at her at the time weren't you?
- I don't think it was all your fault. We all have a point of no return and she caused you to enter yours. True?"

Arson Investigation

"I turned off the hard-top road, got out of the car and left it running. I reached in and dropped it in gear, steering it over the hill. The car went way over an embankment. I walked down and shut the car off. I removed the keys and soaked the whole car in gasoline. I took a cigarette lighter and lit it. I took off back up the steep hill."

"I caught a ride with someone on the hard-top road, but I'm not sure who it was. I'm not sure where I went right after that, but I ended up at my house. I really don't remember much more than what I've told you."

What did you notice?

He became vague using fewer perceptual phrases, included negations, and passive voice.

I turned off the hard-top road, got out of the car and left it running (touch). I reached in and dropped it in gear, steering it over the hill (touch). The car went way over an embankment (sight). I walked down and shut the car off (touch). I removed the keys and soaked the whole car in gasoline (touch). I took a cigarette lighter and lit it (touch). I took off back up the steep hill (touch).

I caught a ride with someone (vague or passive voice) on the hard-top road, but I'm not sure (negation, lack of knowledge) who it was.

I'm not sure (negation, lack of knowledge) where I went right after that, but I ended up at my house. I really don't remember (negation, lack of memory) much more than what I've told you.

Statement of man accused of rape

"I put her clothes on and, um, and she and I walked outside and said our good-byes. I gave her a hug and told her I had a good time and she talked for a minute and then I left. I walked home."

The suspect did not use the pronoun "we" to describe the two, but, instead, he said, "she and I." In sexual assault cases, especially those where the subject alleges that the sexual contact was consensual, you should listen for the absence of the pronoun "we." This lack of a word suggests that a healthy relationship did not exist between the two individuals and increases the likelihood that the sexual contact was less then consensual. This is the exact opposite situation we saw in the beginning.

The suspect did not state that the woman said that she had a good time; instead, he said, "she and I said our goodbyes," a vague and imprecise comment. In addition, he stated that "she talked." The statement suggests that a lot of conversation occurred, thus you should focus your line of questioning there. Some follow up questions could be:

• You said that "she and I said our good-byes." What did you mean by this? What exactly was said by her and then by you?

• You told her that you had a good time. What precisely did you tell her? Tell me exactly what you said.

• Did she ever state that she also had a good time? What did she have to say about the sexual relations? How did she feel about it?

• You said that "she talked for a minute and then I left." What exactly did she talk about? What words did she use? After she talked, you then left. What happened before you left? Why did you leave? Why did you go home? What did you do when you got home?

Following the rape, the suspect attempted to apologize to her for what he had done and even tried to give her a hug, which she rejected. The victim had advised investigators that she told the assailant that she was going to report the rape to the police and that he tried to get her to reconsider before he left in tears.

Look at the last part of his statement, "she talked for a minute and then I left. I walked home." He used a text bridge "then" which creates a time loss which we later learn. She was going to report the rape to the police and that he tried to get her to reconsider before he left in tears. He could not retell that part because it shows her feelings of rape and calling the police and his pleading with her not to.

A woman's open ended question to what she did today

"I got up around 6 a.m. while he stayed in bed. He came down about 8 a.m., and he and I talked. I then left to pick up my partner, Stan, about 8:20. Met Stan and we chatted the whole way. We got to our rooms at 2 p.m., and I started to get cleaned up. That's about it."

Tell me what you see in this statement?

She never introduces the first person she spoke to. She said "he and I talked" but she "chatted" with Stan. We later discover that the first person was her husband whom she was having arguments and having an affair with Stan. "That's about it" in closing tells us there is certainly more.

"While Darin was gone, the boys brought down their blankets and pillows and asked if they could watch TV. I said yes. Darin came home and sat down with us while we watched TV. Soon after that, the boys both fell asleep. We talked about a few problems that we were having with the car and the boat and had a few words between us. I told Darin that I was desperate because I had not been able to take the boys anywhere because we only had one car."

Tell me what you see in this statement?

"Darin came home and sat down with us while we watched TV. " She never indicated that her husband actively participated with them in watching television, a social encounter often used to conceal verbal interaction.

You could ask,

   • "Tell me about your husband sitting down "with us while we watched TV."

      • What were you watching?

      • Who was the "we" that watched TV?

      • Did your husband watch TV with you? What did the two of you talk about while the boys watched TV?

Parents often wait until their children cannot hear them before engaging in a serious conversation. In fact, after her sons fell asleep, her words suggested that the exchange with her husband became tense.

      • What were the "few problems" you talked about?

      • What did you mean by "We...had a few words between us"?

"I was at home with my girlfriend and ate dinner around 6:00pm. We watched TV for a while then she left. I then watched TV until midnight."

      • What did you eat and did you both eat together?

      • Can you remember the exact time that you ate?

      • What time did you start and finish watching TV?

- What time did she leave?

- What time did you start watching TV again?

All of the time gaps must be filled in in order to see the entire picture of the statement.

Episode Markers - 11

Researchers Isabel Picornell and Jack Schafer have independently developed different approaches to SA. They study linguistic patterns in people to help identify fraud. At a minimum, a narrative contains 2 clauses, the reportable events (what happened) and temporal separation (the time separating the earlier from the later events). Fully formed narratives have a beginning, middle, and an end. Narrators use segmentation markers as signals to manage the flow and understanding of information. They are deliberate and divide narratives into separate episodes to draw attention to change and to areas considered important. Deviation from the standard sentence construction of main clause + subordinate clause to that of subordinate clause + main clause can be significant.

Examples:

The ambulance arrived moments later.

Moments later, the ambulance arrived.

We met with a group of friends once we got to the movie theatre.

Once we got to the movie theatre, we met with a group of friends.

Language is influenced by the author's focus, and that focus is in turn managed by the author's intentions. The finished product (the deception) is a compilation of the deceiver's intention (to tell the truth or to lie) and choice of communication strategy to achieve that intent.

Episode markers are important as they are subconscious markers of the narrator to break the continuity of the statement. Excessive fragmentation is associated with artificial timelines. When a sequence of events is imagined or gaps in time occur, the continuity of the narrative breaks down. Narratives fragment into multiple short episodes because the events described are not anchored in real time. They are created with punctuations and words like: ___and, when, then, but.___

We can use episode markers in a statement to break it down from before, during and after, but further with each episode. (Changes in time, place or markers) The shorter or more plentiful are episode markers, the greater the likelihood of their non-commit to the statement.

He grabbed me and held a knife to my throat. And when I woke up and I was, I mean I was really asleep and I didn't know what was going on, and I kind of you know I was scared and I kind of startled when I woke up, you know, you know I was startled and he, he told, he kept telling me to shut up and he asked me if I could feel the knife.

{He grabbed me} and {held a knife to my throat.} And {when I woke up} and {I was}, {I mean I was really asleep} and {I didn't know what was going on,} and {I kind of you know I was scared} and {I kind of startled when I woke up,} {you know,} {you know I was startled} and {he,} {he told,} {he kept telling me to shut up} and {he asked me if I could feel the knife.}

There are two types of strategies which have been identified in narratives; 1) wordy and personal 2) impersonal.

1) Wordy and personal use of a lot of words and can appear important, yet are vague and utilize an excessive number of pronouns like *I*, *me*, and *my*. Me and my represent passive pronouns and should be watched.

Verb strings are also indicative of deceptive issues. Verb strings are 2 or more verbs that function as a verb (went to call, started yelling, tried to open).

Cognitive verbs or cognitive functions like *think*, *appear*, and *seem* are short cuts and not based in emotion.

Indefinite pronouns which refer to something or someone unspecified are also known as passive voice words. *something*, *someone*,

Watch for conjunctions that join a negation to an assertion: "I was in the vehicle, but I was *not* aware of what was going on."

Watch for excessive adverb/adjective use.

In the sentence "I do not remember seeing someone behind me" contains a Negation (not), a Cognitive Verb (remember), a Verb String (remember seeing), and a passive voice (someone).

Analyze the next paragraph:

He grabbed me and held a knife to my throat. And when I woke up and I was, I mean I was really asleep and I didn't know what was going on, and I kind of you know I was scared and I kind of startled when I woke up, you know, you know I was startled and he, he told, he kept telling me to shut up and he asked me if I could feel the knife.

2) impersonal strategies are when deceivers become increasingly other oriented resulting in a high use of third person (he, she, they, we, us) and prefer to be absent by replacing I with me or my.

Then **he** told **me** to stop crying. **He** told **me** to stop the car. **He** took tape out and put it on **my** wrists.

People remember what they said, not how they said it. Memory is not stored in verbal form. We do not remember:

- Slang & non-standard grammar forms: gonna, gimme, buddy
- Acknowledgements: yeah, okay, sure
- Fillers: like, you know what I mean, sort of
- Adverbial modifiers: just, really, very

When two texts are very similar, it is more likely that one has been "borrowed" from another text rather than the same speaker creating them independently. They still have to decide how to convey the false account in a way that will appear balanced and consistent with the known truths; without feedback, deceivers have to guess as to how best to structure their deception so as to appear truthful and convincing.

Mental Dictionary, Balance, and Emotions - 12

The exact size of the mental dictionary is not known, although it is estimated that there are about 30,000 words in our vocabulary. Research calculates that with an average rate of speech of 150 words per minute, peaking at approximately 300 words per minute, the average speaker has 200—400 milliseconds to select the words they wish to use. Expressed another way:

2 to 5 times a second we have to make the right choice from those 30,000 words. It is estimated that the probability of making the wrong choice is one in a thousand. Formulae make the business of speaking (and that of hearing) easier. When a speaker uses a formula they need to retrieve it from the dictionary instead of building it up from its basic parts. In other words, such expressions exist as whole or partial statements within the speaker's dictionary and need not be built up from scratch on every new occasion.

A story, like most things in life, requires balance. It has been found that a balanced story is suggestive of truth. This balance is shown as:

- Prologue (introduction) 20%
- Event (incident) 50%
- Epilogue (conclusion) 30%

To assist in this determination, draw a border around the criminal incident section and glance at the entire statement to see the lengths of each section. For a more accurate balance, calculate the word count percentage of each section by dividing the total number of words in the statement into the number of words in each section. Examine the word-count percentages of the three sections to determine the lengths of each section. A relatively long prologue may indicate deception. This occurs when the subject is trying to explain why (convince) something happened instead of telling us what (convey) happened.

Significant variations from average sentence length require explanation. A way to do this is to calculate the average sentence length and look for sentences with a large change from the average. Look for excessive descriptors, and change in pronouns and tense. Breaks in logic are indicators of deception. Watch for information balance such as is there too much or too little information. Everything in the statement needs relevance. Everything in the narrative must be relevant to something else in the narrative and the narrative must, overall, be relevant to the episode. The categories of this relevance include time, place, and so forth.

Truthful statements will have more affective statements involved or statements about feelings. In a traumatic event, these emotions will spill out in the epilogue or conclusion of the statement. It is not until a traumatic event concludes that we will see the inclusion of emotion because this is when they occur.

A victim of a quickly occurring traumatic event may not be aware of emotions until the trauma ends. Truthful victims may include specific descriptions of fear, anger, embarrassment, or shock in their conclusions. Because emotions in the conclusion reveal the crime's effect on the writer, the presence of emotions may provide a clue that the event actually was experienced, not fabricated.

A bank robbery getaway driver wrote that she "was nervous and scared" and "heard a gunshot and jumped because it scared me." The descriptions of fear in her written statement indicated that the incident described likely did happen and it did not traumatize her..

A rape victim concluded her statement with: "I was hysterical and locked all the doors." The location of the emotion inclusion is important. During a traumatic event, we will not experience emotion until it is over. This is all part of our autonomic nervous system. In these examples, the trauma of the rape victim was properly in the end while the scared driver included it within.

I am often asked how we can use these strategies in court. Dr Picornell said it best with her advice that reports gathered and constructed using forensic linguistics should not be used as principal evidence in court — for now — but only as supporting evidence.

Transitional Words & Phrases - 13

Using transitional words and phrases helps papers read more smoothly, and at the same time allows the reader to flow more smoothly from one point to the next. Transitions enhance logical organization and understandability and improve the connections between thoughts. They indicate relations, whether within a sentence, paragraph, or paper.

A Comprehensive List of Adverbial Conjunctions and Their Functions

Addition - again, also, then, besides, equally important, finally, first, further, furthermore, in addition, in the first place, last, moreover, next, second, still, as well as, coupled with, in addition, likewise, similarly

Comparison - also, in the same way, likewise, similarly

Concession - granted, naturally, of course

Contrast - although, yet, at the same time, despite that, even so, even though, for all that, however, in contrast, in spite of, instead, nevertheless, though, notwithstanding, on the contrary, on the other hand, otherwise, regardless, still, but, contrast

Emphasis - certainly, indeed, in fact, of course

Example or Illustration - after all, as an illustration, even, for example, for instance, in conclusion, indeed, in fact, in other words, in short, of course, namely, specifically, that is, to illustrate, thus, truly

Summary - altogether, finally, in brief, in conclusion, in other words, in short, in simpler terms, in summary, on the whole, therefore, to put it differently, to summarize

Consequence - accordingly, as a result, consequently, for this reason, for this purpose, hence, otherwise, so then, subsequently, therefore, thus, thereupon, wherefore

Time Sequence – after a while, afterward, again, also, then, as long as, at last, at length, at that time, before, besides, earlier, eventually, finally, formerly, further, furthermore, in addition, in the first place, in the past, last, lately, meanwhile, moreover, next, now, presently, second, shortly, simultaneously, since, so far, soon, still, subsequently, thereafter, too, until, when, for now, later on, simultaneously.

Transitional Words

Time - after, afterward, before, during, earlier, final, first, later, since, meanwhile, then, until

Contrast - however, in contrast, indeed, instead, nevertheless, on the contrary, on the other hand, yet

Result - As a result, because, consequently, on account of, so, then, therefore, thus, chiefly

Addition or Example - also, besides, for example, furthermore, in addition, moreover

It rained on Saturday; therefore, the picnic was canceled

The idea of it rained was connected to the idea of the canceled picnic with the transitional word, therefore

They can both separate and connect ideas

During the break I drank a soda.

During brings the ideas of a break and drinking a soda together.

We went bowling instead of going to the movies.

The transitional word instead contrasts the act of going bowling and the act of going to the movies.

Subordinating Words

Subordinating words connect unequal but related ideas and create time gaps.

Subordinating words include after, although, as if, as long as, because, before, even though, if, in order that, since, so, that, than, though, unless, until, when, whenever, where, wherever, where, whenever, and while.

Examples:

When there is a trusting relationship coupled with positive reinforcement, the partners will be able to overcome difficult situations.

Highway traffic came to a stop as a result of an accident that morning.

The children were very happy. On the other hand, and perhaps more importantly, their parents were very proactive in providing good care.

She scanned the horizon for any sign though in the distance she could not see the surprise coming her way.

Consensus was arrived at by all of the members then we decided to hold off on the vote.

Some friends and I drove up the beautiful coast <u>chiefly</u> to avoid the heat island of the city.

There were a few very talented artists in the class, <u>but</u> for the most part the students only wanted to avoid the alternative course.

The research was presented in a very dry style <u>though</u> was coupled with examples that made the audience tear up.

In their advertising business, saying things directly was not the rule. <u>That is to say</u>, they tried to convey the message subtly though with creativity.

The music had a very retro sound <u>but</u> at the same time incorporated a complex modern rhythm.

She didn't seem willing to sell the car this week, <u>but</u> in any case I don't get paid until the end of the month.

Example 1

"Did you strike Frank?"

Which of the following sentences are more truthful?

- "Me? Hit someone? Really?"
- "Hitting is not something in my nature."
- "No, I didn't hit him. I wasn't even in town."

Note: In the first two statements: neither uses "I" nor denies the act. If the person responding doesn't deny something expressly, don't supply the express denial for them. The first two statements also are referencing in present tense.

Example 2

"Did you steal $150.00 from the register on Monday?"

- "That missing money isn't my fault."
- "Look, drawers are constantly short, this sort of thing happens all the time."
- "No, I didn't steal anything."

In the first 2 statements, the writer has removed the primary verb steal and replaced it with softer verbs; missing and short. In addition, we do not see the confirming pronoun "I."

Statement made by Steven Avery about his meeting with Teresa Halbach, a photographer for an Auto Trader magazine. She was never seen again after the shoot. Her body was found buried on his property.

"Took a picture, collect the money, and say hi. That's about it."

He does not use any pronouns such as "I", "she", or "we" indicating a lack of commitment. He uses present tense verbs describing a past event; "collect the money" and "say hi". He concludes the statement with the phrase "That's about it" which tells us there is more.

Statement Reviews - 14

I mentioned earlier that I find it easier to break a statement down into separate sentences. This can be broken down even further by chances in time, place or segmentation markers. You can number each separate line for identification purposes to assist in the statement dissection. You will see examples of each in the upcoming section of "Some Well Known Cases."

There is another practice used by UK police forces known as SE3R. SE3R is a mnemonic (memory aid) specifying five steps that help get the most from a particular interview statement. SE3R stands for Survey, Extract, Read, Review, and Recall. The process is as follows:

• Survey - the document is skimmed i.e. read through once at a faster than normal pace

• Extract - the document is gone through systematically, with fine-grain detail (using symbols, abbreviations, etc) being extracted and entered on an 'event line' (which becomes known as the 'SE3R' for ease of purpose)

• Read - document is read at normal speed checking the text against the event line information and making any necessary corrections

• Review - document is set aside and the event line and accompanying information is examined thoroughly for completeness, consistency, clarity and so on

• Recall - the processes involved in producing the SE3R will have ensured much of the material entered the long-term memory, thus making it both familiar and easily recalled. If necessary, specific efforts can be made to ensure all of it is memorized.

The SE3R is designed to:

• Help officers collate witness and suspect accounts for evaluation as part of the investigation process

• Act as an aide to planning further investigation and interviews

• To be used as a reference in further interviews

• Help compare one interviewee's account with that of another

• Help identify gaps, contradictions and so on

• Help evaluate the validity and reliability of the reported information

• Help an investigator communicate the results of interviews or statements to key parties like supervisors and prosecutors.

As we can see, this is an interesting process to assist you in developing a time line with the listed facts. If you utilized this method on each statement that has multiple statements, you can determine if each statement is the same. You could utilize SE3R on one side and our syntax breakdown arraignment of time, place, and segmentation markers. I can see how this could be a very effective combined method of keeping everything straight and understanding both who needs to be re-interviewed and what parts of the statements should be readdressed.

Epilogue

I understand that much of this material can be confusing. There is a lot to cover in a short amount of time. Your comprehension of the techniques will fade a little each day without review and use. There is a forgetting curve. The forgetting curve works on the principle that we forget remembered topics continually. It occurs faster in the beginning as our brains make room for ideas introduced. In fact, by the end of the first day after learning new information, we will lose 50-80 percent of that information unless reviewed. However, by reviewing the learned information within 24 hours, you have told your brain that the material is important and needs to be remembered. Your brain responds by not allowing this memory from being pushed out too quickly. One week later, if you will review the material again, you are sealing it within your own mental computer. Afterwards, a review every 30 days should suffice for you to remember the information well.

As with everything in our toolbox, we must use them or they begin to oxidize and rust. None of these techniques will work 100% of the time, on 100% of the people, in 100% of the situations. Therefore, to become an effective interviewer, you must be able to recognize when one technique is failing and be prepared to attempt another with the same confidence. This requires study and use. Some people excel at lying and you must be just as good at their detection.

As I said in the beginning, take as many courses that are available to you and read as many books as possible on these topics. If you can learn just one thing from any book or class, it was a great book or class. You have been able to add another tool to your toolbox. The more tools in the toolbox, the better prepared you become for any task.

If you did not notice, I intentionally made my Prologue (introduction) and Epilogue (conclusion) about the same size to give this book balance. It is a reminder to not forget that every story must have a beginning, a body, and an end.

Some Well Known Cases

1.   "Mr. Ramsey.

2.   Listen carefully! We are a group of individuals that represent

3.	a small foreign faction. We xx respect your bussiness

4.	but not the country that it serves. At this time we have

5.	your daughter in our posession. She is safe and unharmed and

6.	if you want her to see 1997, you must follow our instructions to

7.	the letter.

8.	You will withdraw $118,000.00 from your account. $100,000 will be

9.	in $100 bills and the remaining $18,000 in $20 bills. Make sure

10.	that you bring an adequate size attache to the bank. When you get

11.	home you will put the money in a brown paper bag. I will call you

12.	between 8 and 10 am tomorrow to instruct you on delivery. The

13.	delivery will be exhausting so I advise you to be rested. If we

14.	monitor you getting the money early, we might call you early to

15.	arrange an earlier delivery of the money and hence a earlier

16.	delivery pickup of your daughter.

17.	Any deviation of my instructions will result in the immediate

18.	execution of your daughter. You will also be denied her remains

19. for proper burial. The two gentlemen watching over your daughter

20. do not particularly like you so I advise you not to provoke them.

21. Speaking to anyone about your situation, such as Police, F.B.I.,

22. etc., will result in your daughter being beheaded. If we catch you

23. talking to a stray dog, she dies. If you alert bank authorities, she

24. dies. If the money is in any way marked or tampered with, she dies.

25. You will be scanned for electronic devices and if any are found, she

26. dies. You can try to deceive us but be warned that we are familiar

27. with Law enforcement countermeasures and tactics. You stand a 99%

28. chance of killing your daughter if you try to out smart us. Follow

29. our instructions and you stand a 100% chance of getting her back.

30. You and your family are under constant scrutiny as well as the

31. authorities. Don't try to grow a brain John. You are not the only

32. fat cat around so don't think that killing will be difficult. Don't

33.   underestimate us John. Use that good southern common sense of yours.

34.   It is up to you now John!

35.   Victory!

36.   S.B.T.C"

Casey Anthony

"I got off of work, left Universal driving back to pick up Caylee like a normal day. And I show up to the apartment knock on door nobody answers. So, I call Zeniada cell phone and it's out of service. It says the phone is no longer in service, excuse me. So, I sit down on the steps and wait for a little bit to see if maybe it was just a fluke if something happened and time passed and I didn't hear from anyone. No one showed up to the house so I went over to J. Blanchard Park and checked a couple of other places where maybe possibly they would have gone; couple stores, just regular places that I know Zenida shops at and she's taken Caylee before. And after about 7:00 when I still hadn't heard anything I was getting pretty upset, pretty frantic and I went to a neutral place. I didn't really want to come home. I wasn't sure what I would say about not knowing where Caylee was still hoping that I would get a call or you know find out that Caylee was coming back so that I could go get her. And I ended up going to my boyfriend Anthony's house who lives in Sutton Place."

Charlie Rogers

"Being a victim in a situation like this, or a survivor, um, and then having your, uh, integrity questioned I guess, it feels very victimizing again. It feels very, uh, saddening, uh, it makes an already difficult situation more difficult. Um. Because you know my world, has been changed forever by these events and and uh, so that the idea that that people think its a lie so, uh, it's hurtful.

It's understandable, I mean, intellectually, I understand that people sort of have a hard time wrapping their heads around the events that have happened as do I.

Um, but I'm a person, you know. With feelings, with concerns and just so uh, it feels like I don't know, like a punch in the stomach, kinda. Like a betrayal.

Instead of the focus being on safety and healing and the investigation the whole things turned into a defense and it starts to feel like, oh, you know like, you know it doesn't even become about the situation. It becomes something about all together different and then I started to feel like a pawn in a game. That isn't my game, you know. This isn't, you know, I didn't ask for this, I don't want this, and so you know the, I , whatever peoples intentions are or are not, um, it is important to me that they understand, for myself and future victims, hopefully there will be none but.

People are people. Agendas are agendas and I think that this is so important that we distinguish between those two things. Um. I was hurt. And, like what matters is the story. You know? That's awful. It feels awful to me. This is an investigation. This is a crime. This is not, it deserves a level of respect. I know when these sorts of things happen, it, it ignites fires and that's a good thing, in some ways, um, it can also be a very bad thing. Um.

I'm not a pawn in a game, you know. I'm a person and it very much feels like I'm being used as a pawn. I want people to know I'm not afraid. I want other victims to know that it is important to come forward. I also wanted some control over what was happening in the media. Um. And I though that the best way to do that was to do it myself. I want people to understand. Maybe you don't know me.

But you probably know somebody that something like this has happened to. So, for people to think that this doesn't happen here; it does. It did.

Everyone is worthy of safety, of justice and of fairness and I'm not hiding from this anymore. There is fear, but there is resilience, you know, there is, forward."

Jim Ragsdale

Since it was the Fourth
of July weekend, I had
several days off work.
I was working driving a
truck, transporting
heavy equipment for a
gas line. My girlfriend
was from Las Cruces,
and I lived in Carlsbad.
We decided to go to
the perfect place near
Boy Scout Mountain in
a campsite where we
would have solitude.
We went up Pine Lodge
Road and turned onto a
gravel road heading
toward the campsite.
We went where there is
a picnic grounds and
we had access to water.
I parked my pickup
behind a clump of
trees, got the quilts out
and put them in the
back of my pickup, and
we started drinking
beer and making
out. We were lying in
the back of my pickup
truck, buck naked,
drinking beer,

and having a good ole
time when about 11:30
the night of July 4,
1947, all hell broke
loose. From the
northwest, there was a
big flash, an intense,
bright explosion,
and then, shortly
thereafter, with a noise
like thunder, this thing
came plowing through
the trees, shearing off
the tops, and then
stopped between two
huge rocks. It was
propped up against one
rock. It was about
twenty feet around. As
it was approaching,
huge streams like fire
were coming out from
behind. After the
mpact, silence.
The damn thing
stopped about sixty
yards from the pickup,
and we thought at first
it was going to hit us.
After the impact, we
were scared, but
curious. We went down
to the crash of this disc-
like thing. There was a
hole in one side about
four feet wide and two
feet high. There was

66

junk scattered around the disc, and we picked some of it up. I looked inside the hole, and inside, there was a chair that looked like a throne. It looked like it was made of rubies and diamonds. There were other little chairs Ð four or five and a lot of instruments on a panel. There were also the little people, four of them. They looked like midgets, about four feet long. Their skin, if it was skin, was sort of gray and when I touched one of them, it felt like a wet snake. How on earth did this thing fly, I wondered. All around the bottom of the capsule were little wheels that had more wheels. I figured these had to have something to do with how it maneuvered and flew. The captain's chair was something else. It was beautiful. Several hours later, we went back to see the disc in daylight. Shortly afterwards, my

girlfriend and I heard a
siren and trucks
coming. We picked up
some of the trash
around the crash, and
headed back to our
campsite. The campsite
was in a secluded area
and we watched as
many military vehicles
pulled up to the crash.
We decided to get the
hell out of there.
Several days later, I
went to the Blue Moon.
That was a popular
tavern back then. We
showed some of the
debris to some of my
buddies. They are all
dead now. My girlfriend
went back to Las Cruces
and took some of the
material with her. She
died in an alleged car
accident pretty soon
after, and the crash
stuff was never found.
My house was broken
into, and the only
things that the thieves
stole was a pistol and
all of the debris I had
picked up at the crash.
From that time until
today, I was afraid;
afraid for the safety of

my family, knowing
that many had been
threatened by officials
in the military.

JODI ARIAS

Police Interviews

DF – Detective Flores

JA – Jodi Arias

_____ are breaks in the complete statement

Pre-Attack

DF: Were you at Travis's house on Wednesday?

JA: Absolutely not! I was nowhere near Mesa. I was nowhere near Phoenix.

JA: I wasn't even close to him. Umm

DF: What if I can show you proof you were there? Would you change your mind?

JA: I wasn't there!

DF: Be honest with me, Jodi.

JA: I was not at Travis's house. I was not...

DF: There's so much evidence in that house. So much... and it all points to you.

JA: I...I lived there. I was there for months and months and months.

DF: Mmm Hmm. I know you took pictures of him in the shower, just before he died.

JA: I don't think he would allow that...

DF: Mmm Hmm...and the camera actually took a couple of photos by accident during the time he was being killed.

JA: Really?

DF: We have your blood at the scene...your hair with blood at the scene...your left palm print at the scene, in blood. What's going on there?

JA: Well, I can explain the blood and the hair. I don't know about my left palm print.

DF: How can you explain the blood and the hair?

JA: Well, because I used to bathe Napoleon all the time and... umm

----

DF: Jodi... Jodi... This is over. This is absolutely over. You need to tell me the truth.

JA: Listen, the truth is I did not hurt Travis. Okay, so...

DF: Jodi! You can continue to do this, okay? The records show that you reported a gun stolen... a 25 auto. This happens to be the same caliber as the weapon used to kill him.

JA: A 25 auto was used to kill Travis?

JA: Listen, if I'm found guilty, I don't have a life. I'm not guilty. I didn't hurt Travis. If I hurt Travis, if I killed Travis, I would beg for the death penalty.

DF: Was there anybody else with you?

JA: I was traveling alone. The whole time

DF: Was there anybody else with you at Travis's house on Wednesday the 4th?

JA: I was not at Travis's house on Wednesday the 4th.

DF: You were, because that's when the blood was left on... the bloody palm print was left on his wall. I don't know what to tell you. If you were in my shoes and I had this evidence against... against you, what would you say?

JA: If I had that evidence against you?

DF: Yeah!

JA: It would be pretty obvious, but I guess being in my position I'd ... it just seems so impossible. I'd want to see it, I'd want to know, I mean...I'm not like.. I'm not a murderer but I guess if I were to do that I'd wear gloves, or, you know, something. I just...How can my... I don't' know...

Different Interview – The Attack

DF: What happened when the last picture was taken?

JA: He was kneeling down in the shower. I don't remember.

(Jodi becomes animated and begins to use her hands/body to demonstrate)

JA: He's like...if this is the shower and the sink is over here, I was like right here taking pictures, and I don't really know what happened after that exactly, except I think he was shot.

DF: Where were you?

(Jodi becomes animated during this response, gets up from her chair and begins to demonstrate where everything was in Travis' bathroom. She proceeds to kneel on the floor to show Detective Flores where she was crouched)

JA: Umm... if this is his shower and he was sitting here, I was like...Well, if this is his shower, and he's sitting here, I was like right there on my knees, and his bathtub was right here, and I was taking them here, and I was just going through the pictures, and I heard this loud ring,

(Jodi gets up and sits back in her chair. Jodi pulls both of her feet up onto the edge of the chair seat, positioned such that her entire body is on the seat of the chair, knees level with her shoulders)

JA: and...I don't really remember except Travis was screaming. I think I got knocked out, but I don't think I was out long. I know I got knocked in the head, and I've gotten knocked in the head once by my dad when he was just really mad, and it wasn't like... Actually, he didn't knock me in the head, he just pushed me against the wall, and I hit my head and I fell, but he...In this case I think it was similar because he uh... was screaming, and I was by the bathtub, and he was holding his head, and there were two people there and...

JA: I was like, "Are you okay? What's going on? What's going on?" and he's like, "Go get help! Go get help!" and I said, "Okay!" I turned around. There were two people there, one was a guy and one was a girl. I couldn't tell that at first, but you could see one was a girl and one was a guy because of their build and their voices. Um...I remember what they were wearing like maybe jeans, um...

DF: What did they say?

73

JA: One was in all black and one was in jeans.

DF: Did they say anything?

JA: Yeah, the girl wanted to kill me, too.

DF: What did she say? What words did you hear? What phrases?

JA: Umm…"Who is that? Who is that?" I thought he was by himself or alone or something and… He was like, "Shut up, just finish it," and Travis was screaming the whole time. He wasn't screaming like a girl. He was just like… like he was in pain… like he was like shocked, like "Ahhhh," you know. He wasn't really moving though, you know, he was just kind of staying still on the floor.

DF: Then what happened?

JA: Well, as soon as he said, "Go get help," I turned around and they were there and…

Umm…she was over him and I just rushed her and I pushed her, and there was…

DF: There was what?

JA: Travis was bleeding everywhere.

DF: What was she doing to him, because he had been shot at this time, right?

JA: Yeah, but he was still alive.

DF: Mmm hmm.

JA: He was conscious even, like…

DF: Still talking…

JA: Oh, he wasn't talking or saying much, but I could tell he was breathing. He seemed like he was breathing calmly, I think, he

74

wasn't like...He was just there. I can't really remember. It was such a blur.

DF: Okay, so what happened after you pushed her?

JA: Um...I got Travis, and he wasn't like standing up really. He wasn't really doing much, and he was... I was trying to get him... and she came back. I got him kind of far, like right here. She came back and uh...He was just... He was starting to just get weaker and weaker, and this guy came back in, and she said that umm...She said... they needed to um....do me, too, because umm.. because I was there, and he was like, "No, that's not why we're here," and...Um...

(DF's phone buzzer goes off)

JA: He had my purse, which I had on the dresser here prior. Umm...

DF: And what did they do after this, after you guys reached this. Just try to stick with the incident from what was going on?

JA: She came after me, and he stopped her.

DF: Okay.

JA: And she didn't get me.

DF: How was she going to get you? Did she have a weapon?

JA: She had a knife.

DF: Okay.

DF: You said she had a gun before.

JA: I don't know if she had a gun. I...I think...'cause I am guessing. Umm...I know that he had a gun. I don't know if she had a gun or not.

DF: So she was basically the aggressor?

JA: Yeah, unless he took a shot, too. I don't know.

JA: No, but it was obvious they were there for him. They didn't say why.

DF: So it seemed like they knew him, obviously.

JA: Yeah, but he didn't seem to know them. I mean he was a little out of it, plus they had masks on anyway, but he didn't express any kind of recognition.

DF: Well, he couldn't talk.

JA: Umm...so I wasn't sure. I just knew I had to hold onto her hands because she had a knife.

DF: What hand did she have it in?

JA: She...she had it in this hand, but well, her right, so...

DF: Her right?

DF: What happened?

DF: So you didn't see her hurt him anymore. He was just bleeding. Where did he end up?

DF: Was that when you left?

JA: He said, "Leave now," and part of me didn't want to leave. Travis wasn't... was still alive. He was still... I could...He wasn't moving a lot, but he was still alive. I could see that he was still...

DF: Did you get hurt at all? You said you were fighting with her.

76

JA: Yeah.

DF: What happened to you?

JA: Umm...she cut me.

DF: Where at?

JA: My hand.

DF: Let me see. Where at? Can you show me?

JA: (Gestures with her left hand) You actually can't see it. If you look at... my finger isn't the same, though. I was...

DF: Let me see. Where did it get cut?

(Jodi extends her left arm and places it on the table. DF gets up and looks closely at her fingers)

JA: It was...Conveniently it was right on the crease.

DF: Okay, so like right in that crease that you... across both of them?

JA: Uhh...not my middle finger, I mean it cut this one a little but not as much. This is where it really went in. I don't know how it happened that all of these other fingers were missed but this one, I don't know. This one, I still can't close this finger all the way. This is as closed as it goes whereas this one goes like that, so my CTR ring used to fit both fingers, and I can't get it on this finger anymore.

Did you see any other cars in the driveway or on the street?

JA: Umm...

DF: Any vehicle descriptions you can give us?

JA: Uhh... no. No, not that I...Not that I...I don't think his roommates were home.

Jeffery MacDonald

The beginning of his initial interview:

"Let's see. Monday night my wife went to bed, and I was reading. And I went to bed about, somewhere around 2:00. I really don't know. I was reading on the couch and my little girl Kristy had gone into bed with my wife. And I went in to go to bed, and the bed was wet. She had wet the bed on my side, so I brought her in her own room. And I don't remember if I changed her or not; gave her a bottle and went out to the couch 'cause my bed was wet. And I went to sleep on the couch. And then the next thing I know I heard some screaming, at least my wife, but I thought I heard Kimmie, my oldest daughter, screaming also and I sat up. The kitchen light was on and I saw some people at the foot of the bed. So, I don't know if I really said anything or I was getting ready to say something. This happened real fast. You know, when you talk about it, it sounds like it took forever, but it didn't take forever. And so, I sat up and at first I thought I was - I just could see three people and don't know if I - if I heard the girl first, or I think I saw her first. I think two of the men separated sort of at the end of my couch, and I keep - all I saw was some people really. "

Bibliography

Adams, Susan (April 2003). COMMUNICATION UNDER STRESS: INDICATORS OF VERACITY AND DECEPTION IN WRITTEN NARRATIVES.

FBI Law Enforcement Bulletin; January 2008, Volume 77, Number 1; Interview Clues by Vincent A. Sandoval

FBI Law Enforcement Bulletin; October 2004, Volume 73, Number 10: Are You Telling Me the Truth? Indicators of Veracity in Written Statements By Susan H. Adams, Ph.D., and John P. Jarvis, Ph.D

FBI Law Enforcement Bulletin; January 2008, Volume 77, Number 1; Text Bridges and the Micro-Action Interview by John R. Schafer

McClish, Mark (2011). 10 Easy Ways To Spot A Liar: The best techniques of Statement Analysis, Nonverbal Communication and Handwriting Analysis.

Picornell, Isabell, 2013. THE FLEXIBLE LIAR: A STRATEGY FOR DECEPTION DETECTION IN WRITTEN WITNESS STATEMENTS

Picornell, Isabell, 2013. Cues to Deception in a Textual Narrative Context

Schafer, John A. 2007. Content Analysis of Written Statements

Sapir, A. 1987. Scientific Content Analysis(SCAN). Laboratory of Scientific Interrogation. Phoenix, AZ.

Sapir, A. 1995. The View Guidebook: Verbal Inquiry – the Effective Witness. Laboratory of Scientific Interrogation. Phoenix, AZ.

Schollum, Mary. September 2005, Investigative interviewing: THE LITERATURE, Office of the Commissioner of Police, PO Box 3017 Wellington NZ

Statement Analysis Presentation, Patrick J Kelly.

http://www.statementanalysis.com/cases/

http://www.lsiscan.com/reports.htm

http://crimeandclues.com/2013/03/02/statement-analysis-what-do-suspects-words-really-reveal/5/

http://seamusoriley.blogspot.com/

http://www.hwprosandcons.com/Statement_Analysis.html

http://www.psychologytoday.com/blog/let-their-words-do-the-talking/201103/text-bridges

http://www2.fbi.gov/publications/leb/1996/oct964.txt

About the Author

Steven Varnell is a law enforcement training specialist who retired after serving over 29 years with the Florida Highway Patrol. During his career he worked Patrol, Field Training, Criminal Interdiction, SRT, and K9. He has instructed Firearms, Baton, Felony Stops, and Criminal Interdiction Courses. He was an adjunct instructor for the MCTFT Program at St. Petersburg College where he taught Highway Interdiction, Officer Safety, Patrol, and Interviews and Interrogation classes for law enforcement agencies throughout the country. He was a part of FHP's criminal interdiction pilot program which began in 1983, where he served in interdiction and K9 duties for 27 year making him one of the most experienced interdiction officers in the country.

Steve is the author of *Criminal Interdiction, Tactical Survival*, and *Behavior Analysis and Interviewing Techniques (BAIT)*, three widely acclaimed books available through bookstores everywhere. He is a sought out instructor and speaker in the officer safety field. Steve has a lecture company called Interdiction and Survival Strategies (ISS), where with former partners, together they have established a new approach to criminal based training. Steve can be reached at criminalinterdiction@live.com or go to his website at criminalinterdiction.yolasite.com. For more information and training information on the ISS group, go to: isspolicetraining.com.

Printed in Great Britain
by Amazon